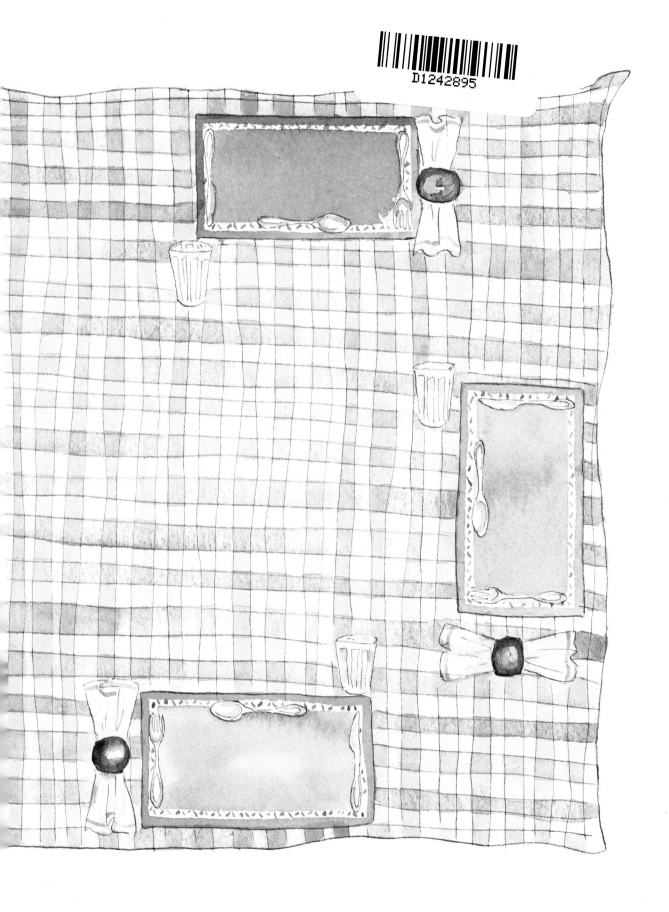

Published by Doubleday, a division of
Bantam Doubleday Dell Publishing Group, Inc.
666 Fifth Avenue, New York, New York 10103

Doubleday and the portrayal of an anchor with a dolphin
are trademarks of Doubleday, a division of
Bantam Doubleday Dell Publishing Group, Inc.

Library of Congress Cataloging-in-Publication Data
Gedye, Jane.
Dinner's ready!: a pig's book of table manners/written and
illustrated by Jane Gedye.—1st American ed.
p. cm.
Summary: A fastidious rabbit and a slovenly pig demonstrate
mealtime dos and don'ts.
1. Dinners and dining—Juvenile humor.   2. Table etiquette—
Juvenile humor.   3. Wit and humor, Juvenile.
[1. Table etiquette.]   I. Title.
PN6231.D647G44   1989
818'.5402—dc 19   88-23691
CIP
AC
ISBN 0-385-26083-0
ISBN 0-385-26084-9 (lib. bdg.)

PRINTED IN BELGIUM
MAY 1989
FIRST AMERICAN EDITION

Dinner's Ready!

A PIG'S BOOK OF TABLE MANNERS

WRITTEN AND ILLUSTRATED BY

Jane Gedye

DOUBLEDAY

NEW YORK   LONDON   TORONTO   SYDNEY   AUCKLAND

Remember to wash your hands,

and don't bring toys to the table.

Use your knife and fork properly.

Wait until everyone has been served before you begin.

Don't reach across the table.

Never talk with your mouth full,

or lick your knife.

Don't play with your food,

or slurp your juice.

Sit in your chair.

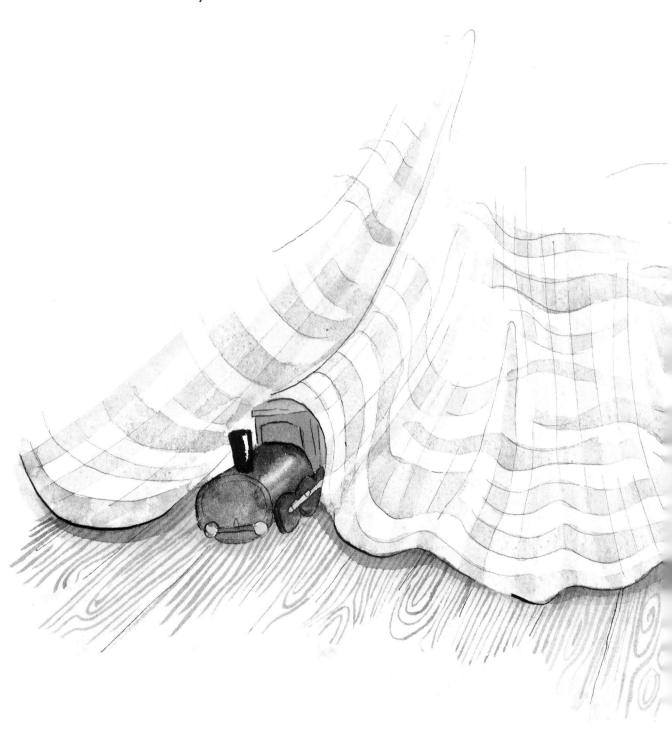

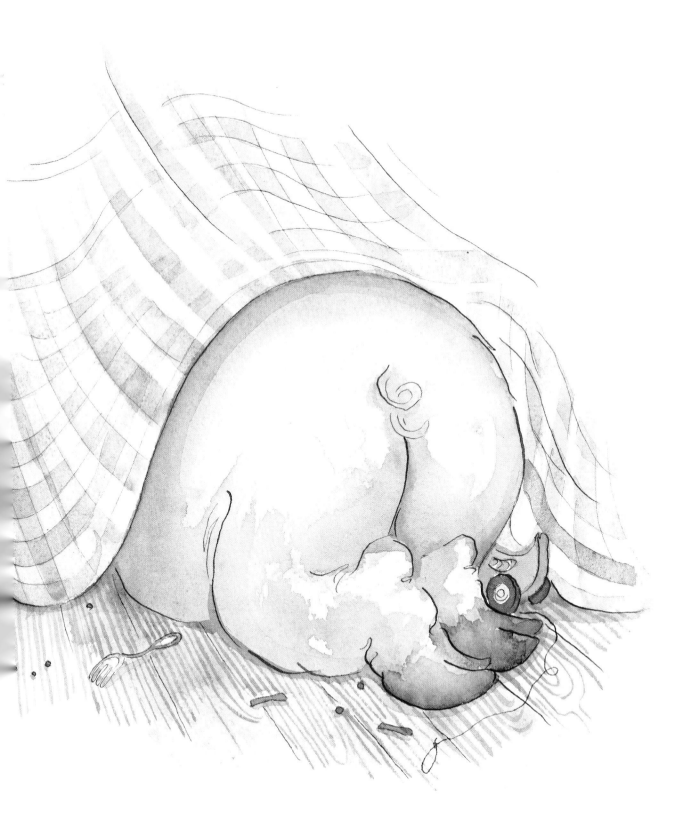

Keep your elbows off the table.

Don't throw food,

or lick your bowl.

Wipe your mouth with your napkin
when you finish.

Ask to be excused before leaving the table.